THE QUIET HABIT OF GIVING
THE QUIET PRACTICES THAT MAKE LOVE LAST

JIM VINCENT

Jim Vincent

The Quiet Habit of Giving

© 2025 Jim Vincent

All rights reserved.

No part of this publication may be reproduced, stored in a retrieval system, or transmitted in any form or by any means—electronic, mechanical, photocopy, recording, or otherwise—without the prior written permission of the publisher, except for brief quotations used in reviews, articles, or scholarly analysis.

This book is intended for personal insight and reflection. It is not a substitute for professional psychological, medical, or legal advice. The author makes no guarantees regarding personal or relational outcomes. Readers should consult appropriate professionals or support services where needed.

This is a work of nonfiction. Every effort has been made to ensure accuracy. Any errors are the responsibility of the author. Opinions expressed are the author's own and do not represent any organization or institution.

Cover design by Jim Vincent.

Published by Vincent Press

Printed in the United States and other countries through authorized print-on-demand services.

First Edition • VP 1.2 • August, 2025

ISBN: 978-1-7641693-7-0

For more information, visit: https://jimvincent.us

For those who kept loving, even after it hurt.

"Love is not something you feel. It is something you do."
— *David Wilkerson*

CONTENTS

Introduction	ix
Preface	xiii
1. A Place to Return to	1
2. What We All Need	3
3. To Be Seen and Not Shrunk	5
4. To Be Included or Forgotten	7
5. To Have a Voice or Be Overruled	9
6. To Grow or Be Held Back	11
7. To Count on Something or Brace For the Storm	13
8. To Know You're Enough or Fear You Are Not	15
9. Love That Pays Attention	17
10. What Hurt Reveals	19
11. When Timing Isn't Enough	21
12. The Quiet Way Love Grows	25
13. Where Love Comes Back	27
14. What Love Remembers	31
Afterword	35
Also by Jim Vincent	41
About the Author	43
Thank You	45

INTRODUCTION

----- ✦ -----

We live in relationship.

Every person we love, every bond we build, every friend we keep, every colleague we trust—each one shapes how we move through the world. The quality of our relationships determines the quality of our days. When they are strong, we breathe easier. When they are strained, the whole world feels tighter. And when they break—suddenly, or slowly—we are left not only with grief, but with a kind of silence. The silence of what was not said. What was not understood. What was not sustained.

We are not often taught how to make a relationship last. We are taught how to begin. How to impress. How to spark affection or stir connection. But we are not given the language to name what holds a bond together. We are not shown what to do when change comes—when someone grows, or falters, or hurts us without meaning to. We are not told how to understand what someone else truly needs, or

INTRODUCTION

how to give it—not once, but repeatedly. We are rarely invited to think of love as something we practise.

But we should be. Because the truth is simple: relationships endure not because of how they start, but because of how they are carried.

This book is about that carrying.

Not just in romantic partnerships, but across all the relationships that matter—friendships, families, marriages, working partnerships, even those still forming or quietly fading. At the heart of all of them are six emotional needs. They are not burdens or signs of weakness. They are the foundations of trust. Admiration. Belonging. Control. Freedom. Security. Validation. Every person needs some of them. Most people need one or two deeply. And when they are present, they nourish. When they are missing, they ache. When they are reversed, they wound.

We don't always know how to speak about them. It can feel self-important to say we need admiration. Needy to say we long to belong. Vulnerable to admit we want validation. So we don't say it. We wait for someone to notice. We hope someone will understand. And when they don't, we grow quiet. Not because we no longer care, but because we feel unseen in a way we don't know how to name.

But these needs are not invisible. They show themselves in how people open. In how they flinch. In what they return to, and in what they defend. And when we learn to watch for them—to recognise the moments that matter, and respond not with performance, but with generosity—something shifts. The bond becomes steadier. Stronger. Safer. Not perfect, but enduring.

This book is not a set of instructions. It is not a formula or a script. It will not tell you how to win someone back or fix something that was never built to last. What it offers is quieter, and maybe more lasting: a way to understand what someone else needs in order to feel safe with you—and how to offer it, again and again, in a way they can actually receive.

The habits you will find here are not loud. They are not flashy. They may go unnoticed when they are working. But they are the habits that hold.

And when they are practised with care—not as strategy, but as rhythm—they make a relationship into something more than chemistry, more than compatibility. They make it into a refuge. A place of return. A place that lasts.

PREFACE

A Relationship That Returned

I am not a relationship expert. I'm a relationship survivor.

I've been married four times. I was also engaged for five years, but we never made it to the altar. That's five long attempts—and five failures. I married young, just twenty-one, and within ten years I had a career and four children. But I had lost touch with my wife, and within five more years, we divorced.

Then came Shelly.

We married and stayed together ten years. And again, it ended. Another marriage followed. Ten years. Another end. Then a long engagement. Another ending. I was beginning to think I wasn't built for this. That maybe I was one of those people who just didn't know how to love well. That maybe connection wasn't something I would ever get right.

But through all of it, I stayed in touch with Shelly. Irregular calls. Birthday greetings. I called her when I got married. And divorced. When I got engaged, and when it ended. She called me when she got married and when she divorced. We

PREFACE

remained close friends. For twenty-two years, we didn't see each other. For nineteen of those years, we lived in different countries. But the thread never broke.

Eventually, we talked about getting back together. The idea came quietly, then gained weight. But I knew one thing with certainty: I wasn't willing to do it unless I could do it differently. If we were going to rebuild this, it had to be for good. And I couldn't walk into the same mistakes hoping for a better result.

So I started asking questions.

What had gone wrong? Not just with Shelly, but with every attempt. What did I keep missing? What did she need that I didn't know how to give? What did I need and never quite name? I wasn't looking for a theory. I was looking for something that worked. Something that wasn't about winning arguments or improving compatibility, but about offering the kind of love that lasts.

That's when I began to notice the pattern.

That's when this book began.

Shelly and I did get back together. We married again. And when she flew to Australia, I wasn't sure I would recognize her in the airport terminal. But I did. And now, eight years later, we are still married—and going strong. We have disagreements. We have fights. But the bond is deeper than it ever was. Stronger. Kinder. Wiser. Happy.

When people ask us why we remarried, we sometimes say we couldn't get the divorce to work. It's a joke, but like most good jokes, it hides something true. Maybe we always hoped —maybe we always knew—we would find our way back. Today, I wear the ring she gave me the first time. She wears the ring I gave her. What broke once didn't disappear. It waited. And when we were ready, we began again—not from scratch, but from experience.

That experience is what shaped this book.

It's not a how-to manual. It's not a list of rules. It's a distillation of what I've learned through failure, repair, and return. These pages are built from the questions I asked when I decided to do it differently—and the answers I found when I started listening more closely, giving more freely, and learning what love actually needs to last.

If you've loved and lost—welcome.

If you're loving now, and hoping to keep it—welcome.

If you've never quite known how to give what someone needed, and want to do better—welcome.

This book is for you.

And for anyone who still believes that love, when offered with care, can come back stronger than before—and stay.

A PLACE TO RETURN TO

────✦────

A relationship is meant to be a place of refuge. Not just from the world, but from performance. A place where it is not risky to be yourself. To grow, to change, to succeed, to fail. To dream, and to change your dreams. To be scared. To be honest. To be fully human. That isn't a luxury—it's the foundation. In a marriage, a friendship, a family, even a team, this kind of refuge is what makes closeness possible.

A true relationship is the one place it should be safe to return to—where you are always welcome. A place to reflect, to restore, to recover. A place to redirect when you're lost, and to rest when you're worn out. A place not just to be seen, but to be received.

But a refuge like that doesn't build itself. It is shaped, slowly, by what we give—and by what we withhold. Not just love in the abstract, but specific, repeatable ways of showing care. And not just kindness, but something deeper: the recognition of what the other person truly needs to feel secure, seen, and whole. Because every lasting relationship is built on six emotional needs. Not luxuries. Not preferences. Needs.

WHAT WE ALL NEED

----✦----

These six needs are: Admiration, Belonging, Control, Freedom, Security, and Validation. When we offer them, the relationship flourishes. When we forget them, it begins to fade. And when we reverse them—replace them with their opposites—we don't just weaken the bond. We do harm. The kind that closes hearts, shuts down honesty, and kills trust.

Each of these six has a mirror. Admiration, when reversed, becomes Criticism. Belonging becomes Exclusion. Control becomes Domination. Freedom becomes Confinement. Security becomes Chaos. Validation becomes Rejection. And when we look closely, we begin to see: nearly every rupture, every wound, every long-unspoken resentment in a relationship can be traced to one of these six reversals.

They are not abstract. They are not decorative. They are the architecture of love—and the blueprint of its undoing.

TO BE SEEN AND NOT SHRUNK

---- ✦ ----

"Admiration expands who we believe we are. Criticism narrows it."
— JP Vincent

*A*dmiration is more than appreciation for what someone does—it is the recognition of who they are. We instinctively say, "Thank you," or "Nice job," but those phrases focus on effort. Admiration goes further. It is saying, "You make people feel safe," or "You have a kind of quiet patience I really respect." It acknowledges presence over performance, character over results. Admiration makes a person feel seen at their core. And when given publicly—when others witness that respect—it deepens the impact. To be admired is not to be flattered. It is to be valued for the way you move through the world.

Criticism is the slow erosion of Admiration. It doesn't always raise its voice. More often, it sighs. It interrupts. It corrects before it affirms. It reaches first for the flaw, then forgets to circle back to the good. It's when "You did it" becomes "Finally," when effort is met with silence, when presence is met with a project. Over time, Criticism doesn't sharpen—it shrinks. It narrows a person's sense of who they are until they begin to believe they are, at their core, a disappointment waiting to be managed.

TO BE INCLUDED OR FORGOTTEN

---- ✦ ----

"Belonging invites. Exclusion isolates."
— JP Vincent

*B*elonging is not simply being part of a group—it is feeling included in the moments that matter. It is being considered, remembered, looped into decisions, asked to join even when the outcome is already set. Many instinctively offer belonging during moments of sadness, but real belonging must also live in everyday joy. It shows up in the saved seat, the spontaneous hug, the look across the room that says, "I'm glad you're here." For some, it also lives in touch: a gentle nudge, a shared laugh, the weight of a hand that says, "You are not alone." Belonging doesn't need a reason. It simply needs practice.

Exclusion is the quiet undoing of Belonging. It rarely announces itself. It doesn't slam the door—it just forgets to open it. It's not being asked, not being informed, not being thought of until it's too late to matter. It's the group photo you weren't in, the dinner no one mentioned, the decision you hear about afterward. It lives in small silences: a conversation that doesn't shift to include you, a glance that doesn't land, a moment of connection where your presence wasn't needed. Over time, Exclusion doesn't just make someone feel left out—it makes them feel unnecessary. Not an afterthought. An absence that no one noticed.

TO GROW OR BE HELD BACK

─ ─ ─ ─ ✦ ─ ─ ─ ─

"Freedom opens possibility. Confinement closes it."
— JP Vincent

Freedom is the right to evolve. To change your mind. To no longer like what you once loved. To dream new dreams. In healthy relationships, Freedom is not granted—it is expected. People are not meant to remain fixed in place. Freedom says, "I want to know who you're becoming, not just who you've been." It does not fear change—it welcomes it. It does not bind someone to their past. It lets them unfold.

Confinement is the refusal to let someone grow. It doesn't always come with rules—it often comes with resistance. A disapproving look when they change their mind. A quiet withdrawal when they shift direction. A subtle message that who they were is who they're required to remain.

Confinement doesn't need a cage. It just needs consequences for becoming. Over time, the person learns that love is conditional—that staying lovable means staying the same. Dreams shrink. Opinions soften. Identity flattens. And the person, once vibrant, begins to disappear.

TO HAVE A VOICE OR BE OVERRULED

---- ✦ ----

"Control fosters trust. Domination undermines it."
— JP Vincent

Control in relationships is not about authority—it is about being granted influence in the spaces that matter. It is being asked where to go, what to watch, what you prefer. And sometimes, it is being allowed to decide. Yielding control is not submission—it is trust. It says, "This matters to you, so I will follow your lead." This is not only about large decisions. Letting someone plan a day, take the reins, or lead the way can be a gift. And often, it is the absence of resistance that matters most—the quiet agreement that someone else's direction is enough.

Domination is the theft of shared Control. It doesn't always look harsh. It often looks like decisiveness, planning, efficiency. But it removes choice. It takes the shared space and makes it a single-person stage. It's always their plan, their timeline, their preference—no matter how politely delivered. Over time, the other person stops voicing input, not out of agreement, but futility. When Control is offered, it fosters trust. When it is seized—especially with a smile—it creates quiet resentment. Domination doesn't always shout. Sometimes it just never asks.

TO COUNT ON SOMETHING OR BRACE FOR THE STORM

---- ✦ ----

"Security reassures. Chaos destabilizes."
— JP Vincent

Security is the quiet certainty that the relationship will hold. Not that it will always be easy, or even stable, but that it will be consistent. That promises matter. That home is a shared commitment, not a performance. It lives in routines, follow-through, the keeping of small agreements. It is built through steadiness in crisis, kindness in conflict, and the predictable reassurance that "we" still exists when things go wrong. Security is not a feeling. It is a history —reliable, unshaken, earned over time.

Chaos is the steady unraveling of Security. It doesn't always look explosive. Sometimes it's just inconsistent. Promises made casually, then forgotten. Moods that shift without warning. The creeping sense that today's "we" might not survive tomorrow's stress. Chaos breaks not by storm, but by erosion. It undoes confidence in the small things—what time someone will arrive, whether they'll follow through, how they'll respond when something goes wrong. Over time, it becomes harder to count on anything. The relationship begins to feel like weather—sometimes sunny, sometimes cold, always unpredictable.

TO KNOW YOU'RE ENOUGH OR FEAR YOU ARE NOT

― ― ― ― ✦ ― ― ― ―

"Validation settles the fear that we are not enough. Rejection confirms it."
— JP Vincent

Validation may be the most misunderstood—and the most essential—emotional need. It isn't about flattery, and it isn't about agreement. It's about reassurance that your worst fears about yourself are not true. That you are not broken, not unworthy, not somehow unacceptable because of a flaw you carry or a mistake you made.

Almost everyone carries some version of that fear. Not smart enough. Not attractive enough. Too loud, too quiet, too much. The fear that people only love you for what you offer—and that when the usefulness fades, so will the love.

Some mask that fear with bravado. Others hide it beneath perfectionism. A few say it plainly, hoping not to be dismissed. But the fear is nearly always there. And validation is what meets that fear—not with denial, but with truth that heals: *"That's not what I see. That's not who you are.*

Validation does not erase mistakes. It simply refuses to redefine the person by them. It acknowledges imperfection but insists that imperfection is not disqualification. It says: *You are, in every shape and size, in every mistake and effort, wholly enough. For me.*

And when that reassurance is absent, something deeper breaks.

Rejection is not always loud. It is not always cruel. More often, it is quiet. A withheld smile. A change in tone. A subtle withdrawal after vulnerability. A joke made at the worst possible moment. A sigh when comfort was asked for. Rejection takes the very fear that someone already holds—and confirms it. *You are too much. You are not enough. You are the problem.*

And because these wounds are old, it rarely takes much. A person who fears being unlovable doesn't need to be yelled at to feel rejected. They just need indifference. Or silence. Or a look that lands too hard. It doesn't matter whether the other person meant it. The fear was already there, waiting.

That is why validation matters. It is not about smoothing over flaws. It is about making sure those flaws do not become definitions. It is about offering someone the one thing their fear insists they'll never receive—unconditional regard.

Validation is what lets people breathe.

And Rejection is what takes the air away.

LOVE THAT PAYS ATTENTION

─ ─ ─ ─ ✦ ─ ─ ─ ─

We all carry one or two needs more deeply than the others. So does every person we care about. Everyone you love, live with, raise, or work beside is shaped by their own quiet longing—the need that most defines whether they feel safe, connected, and whole. And most of the time, they won't tell you what it is. Not because they're secretive, but because it's hard to say out loud.

To admit, "I need to belong," sounds needy.

To say, "I need to be admired," sounds self-important.

To whisper, "I need to be validated," can feel like a confession of weakness.

So they don't say it. They carry it. And they hope—often silently—that someone will see it without needing to be told. And when that hope goes unmet, when the need is overlooked or misunderstood, they don't always protest. They simply retreat. Not because they stopped caring, but because they felt invisible in a way they couldn't explain.

This is where so many relationships begin to fray. Not in cruelty, or betrayal, or even neglect. But in misreading. In the quiet tragedy of two people missing each other because they never learned how to speak what mattered—or how to listen for what was never said.

You don't have to be fluent in every emotional language. But you do have to learn how to observe with care. Begin by watching. Watch for what softens them. What steadies them. What makes them linger in a moment rather than move quickly past it. Watch what they guard, what they protect, what they avoid. The person who stiffens when interrupted may long to feel admired. The one who turns quiet after plans are made without them may carry a deep need to belong.

People show you what they need in the subtlest of ways. They show it through what they remember. Through what they repeat. Through what they defend, and what they seem unable to ask for directly. Your job is not to decode them—it's to care enough to notice.

And once you notice, begin to practice. Not once. Not theatrically. But with rhythm. With warmth. With quiet regularity. You do not need to announce that you see them. You simply show it. And then you show it again.

This is not manipulation. This is not emotional strategy. This is love. And this is how people begin to trust that love will stay. Not because it is grand or poetic or rare, but because it is offered—again and again—in the shape they most need to receive.

WHAT HURT REVEALS

────✦────

*E*ven when you try—when you listen, when you care, when you give your best—you will get it wrong. You'll offer what you would have wanted, not what they needed. You'll act with good intent and still cause pain. You'll say too much or too little, speak too soon or stay silent too long. And in those moments, when your love misses the mark, something important happens: the real need reveals itself.

You don't have to be perfect to love well. But you do have to pay attention after the harm. That moment of tension or retreat, the change in tone or energy—it matters. It tells you something you didn't know before. Not just that you hurt them, but where. And often, what you touched is something far older than the moment itself.

A passing joke that draws a sharp response. A change of plans that creates distance. A gentle correction that's met with silence. These aren't overreactions. They're clues. They tell you: something vital lives here. Something unspoken. Something unguarded.

Most people don't protect what they want. They protect what they need. And the needs we protect most fiercely are often the ones we're ashamed to name. A person who longs for Admiration may laugh off praise but bristle at mild correction. A person who needs Belonging might claim they prefer solitude but ache after being left out. Someone who depends on Validation may mask it with humor, but flinch at the slightest tone of judgment. They're not being fragile. They're being honest, even when they don't know how to say it directly.

If you can learn to read those moments—not defensively, but generously—you begin to see not just the pain, but the pattern. You begin to understand what they couldn't explain. You begin to love them not only through presence, but through recognition.

This is what repair looks like. Not just apology. Understanding. A shift in rhythm. A readiness to do better—not because you failed, but because you care.

Not "I'm sorry you feel that way."
But "I think I see what that touched."
Not "You're overreacting."
But "That mattered. I'll try again."
Hurt is not failure. Hurt is information.
And if you're willing to learn from it—love gets wiser.

WHEN TIMING ISN'T ENOUGH

――――✦――――

Sometimes, love shows up after the moment has passed—not because the feeling wasn't real or the effort insincere, but because the pattern ran too long without change. The need went unmet too many times. The space that once felt like refuge slowly became a place of tension, of second-guessing, of subtle hurt. And eventually, the door that had always been open stopped being opened at all.

Some relationships end in arguments, others in silence, and many simply dissolve beneath the surface. There is no grand break, no definitive moment. Just a slow drift. One person grows tired of asking. The other grows tired of guessing. And the rhythm that once felt effortless now feels forced, heavy, uncertain. The absence begins to speak more loudly than the presence ever did.

Not every relationship can be saved. Not every relationship should be. Some are misaligned from the start—two good people with different instincts, different needs, different languages of care. Others crack under the pressure of neglect, not out of cruelty, but from the wear and tear of repeated misunderstanding. Still others miss their moment—one partner finally ready to repair just as the other gives up trying to be heard. The words come, but the listening has stopped. The map arrives, but the traveler has already left.

And yet, there is something grace-filled in that kind of ending. Because even when a relationship closes, it leaves behind the shape of what mattered. It teaches you. It clarifies. When you understand what you needed and didn't receive, when you can name the absence instead of blaming the entire bond, the story begins to shift. You stop telling yourself you failed at love. You begin to see that you didn't know how to ask. You didn't know what to look for. And now, you do.

You start to recognize the patterns not as flaws in yourself, but as signals. That was Chaos. That was Domination. That was Rejection. It wasn't in your imagination. It wasn't your fault. But now it is yours to name. And with that naming comes the freedom to ask—this time—with clarity.

Some people we love are not ready to be loved in the way they most need. They might not yet know their own longings. Or they may know them, but carry shame about wanting so much. If you try to reach too far, too quickly, even with love in your hands, you may find a wall that was built long before you arrived. That is not failure. That is timing. And timing cannot be fixed by trying harder.

Still, your effort is not wasted.

Because when love comes again—and it will—you will carry something forward. You will know more than you did. You will ask better questions. You will listen with fewer assumptions. You will feel when something is missing and trace it gently. You will stop making yourself small to keep the peace. You will stop blaming others for your confusion. You will recognize what makes you come alive—and what makes you disappear.

And when someone begins to love you in return, you'll meet them not with demands, but with the quiet certainty of someone who knows what they need—and has learned how to give that, too.

That is how the next chapter begins.

Not with perfection.

But with understanding.

With timing.

With truth.

THE QUIET WAY LOVE GROWS

---- ✦ ----

The most enduring relationships are not built on dramatic declarations or rare compatibility. They are built through repetition—through the quiet, consistent offering of what the other person actually needs. This kind of love does not require grand gestures or poetic speeches. It asks for something far more difficult and far more powerful: the willingness to return, again and again, with presence, with care, and with attention.

You admire the person you love—not just in moments of achievement, but in the ordinary, uncelebrated details of their daily life. You include them without waiting to be reminded. You give them influence in the spaces that matter to them. You offer space when they need freedom to think, to breathe, to change. You stay steady when everything else begins to shift. And you remind them they are enough—not because they've earned it, but because you see them fully, and still choose to stay.

These offerings don't always look like love, but they are the very shape of it. They are habits, not declarations. They don't often get celebrated, but they are the difference between connection and collapse. The world teaches us that love is what you feel—that it lives in desire, in longing, in chemistry. But anyone who has lived inside a lasting relationship knows that those things, while beautiful, are not what sustain a bond. Over time, love stops being a feeling and becomes a practice. It becomes something you choose. Something you do.

The most powerful love is not performative. It is not given to prove a point or to impress a crowd. It is the decision to offer what the other person most needs to receive, even when it stretches you, even when it humbles you, even when it costs you your preferred way of showing care. And it becomes love in its truest form only when it is repeated—not once, not perfectly, but reliably. Not because you owe it. Because you want to keep the connection alive.

This practice doesn't diminish you. It doesn't erase your needs or silence your desires. It teaches you how to be generous without disappearing. It teaches you that love is not the loss of self, but the offering of presence. And when two people both learn what the other needs—when they make it a rhythm instead of a performance—they create something rare. The relationship no longer demands constant reassurance. It begins to feel like something you can lean on. Something that softens you. Something that lasts.

That is how love becomes refuge. Not because it is always easy, but because it is always offered.

Not because it never falters, but because it knows how to return.

Not because it is perfect, but because it is practiced.

WHERE LOVE COMES BACK

————✦————

*E*very lasting relationship—whether a decades-long marriage, a hard-won friendship, or a reconciled bond between family members—owes its strength not to perfection, but to repair. It is not sustained by the absence of mistakes, but by the presence of return. We don't love well by never hurting the people we care about; we love well by learning how to come back when we do.

No matter how attentive or well-meaning you are, you will eventually miss the mark. You'll offer what you would have wanted, not what they needed. You'll speak too quickly or stay silent too long. You'll forget a moment that mattered or misread a moment that didn't. And when that happens—when the other person flinches or pulls away or grows quiet—the future of the relationship will not be determined by what went wrong. It will be determined by what happens next.

The people who stay close over time are not those who

never falter. They are the ones who have learned how to recover. They know how to repair without making excuses. They know how to offer presence instead of performance. They understand that an apology is not just an act of regret—it is a commitment to understanding, to adjusting, to restoring what was damaged by carelessness or confusion or stress.

Repair does not require the perfect words. It doesn't ask for ceremony or eloquence. What it does require is sincerity. The ability to look with humility at where we missed, to listen to what mattered, and to offer something better going forward. It asks for the grace to accept imperfection, not as a failure of love, but as the condition of being human.

Over time, this rhythm of return creates its own kind of safety. When someone knows that your presence will come back even after disconnection, that your care doesn't vanish in difficulty, they begin to rest. They begin to trust that they will not lose you the moment they reveal a need, a hurt, or a fault. They begin to believe that love, in your hands, is something they can rely on—even when life or emotion or memory makes the ground unsteady.

This is the work all of this has pointed toward—not simply knowing what people need, not simply avoiding the reversals that wound them, but becoming the kind of relationship that can survive its own mistakes. A relationship where refuge is not just an idea, but a pattern. A daily practice. A place where two people are not perfect, but are willing—again and again—to find their rhythm after it has been lost.

When we make a quiet habit of giving—not grand gestures, not hollow praise, but the actual presence and care someone most needs—we create a bond that can weather life. We build something not only strong, but generous. Not only enduring, but alive. A relationship that does not ask for flawlessness, but for honesty. Not for performance, but for practice. Not for perfection, but for return.

And that, in the end, is what makes the most beautiful relationships what they are. Not their ease. Not their passion. Not even their longevity. What makes them beautiful is the steady, human decision to come back. To notice. To listen. To offer again what matters most, even after we've failed to do so.

A relationship like that isn't found. It is made.

Not once, but every day.

Not through chemistry, but through attention.

Not through instinct, but through care.

It is made by people who have learned that love is not just what you feel. It's what you do—quietly, repeatedly, especially when it would be easier not to.

That is the quiet habit of love.

And it is how we return—not once, but again and again, until returning becomes the rhythm of how we love.

WHAT LOVE REMEMBERS

---- ✦ ----

*I*f you remember nothing else, remember this: every strong relationship rests on six emotional foundations. They are not accessories. They are not seasonal trends. They are not traits of compatibility or coincidence. They are the structure of connection itself.

Admiration. Belonging. Control. Freedom. Security. Validation.

Every person needs some of them. Most people need one or two with particular depth. And when those needs are met, they do more than please us. They heal us. They remind us we are not alone, not invisible, not too much to carry or too strange to love. They root us in something steady and real.

Each of these needs has a reversal—an opposite that wounds where the original would have nurtured. Criticism replaces Admiration. Exclusion takes the place of Belonging. Domination steals Control. Confinement suppresses Freedom. Chaos disrupts Security. Rejection cuts into the place where Validation should have lived. When these patterns show up—not just in isolated moments, but as habits—the bond begins to fray. Even the strongest connection cannot thrive if what's needed is consistently replaced with what harms.

But none of this knowledge is here to accuse. It is here to teach. To open a map. To say: you don't have to guess what love looks like. You don't have to offer what someone else would have wanted. You don't have to keep giving what you were taught to give, hoping it will eventually be enough. You can offer what is actually needed—what brings someone home to themselves and to you.

You can learn what you need. You can carry those six words with you until one or two of them begin to feel like truth. You can look at your memories and notice which need was present when things felt whole, and which one vanished when things fell apart. You can trace your hurts back to their roots and find not failure, but clarity. Not weakness, but insight. That knowledge won't make you fragile. It will make you clear.

And just as you can learn your own, you can learn someone else's. You can watch what quiets them, what opens them, what draws them close. You can notice the patterns in what they return to, what they avoid, what they never quite say, but always seem to feel. You don't need a diagnosis. You need to care enough to notice.

Once you do, you can practise. Not perform. Not perfect. Practise.

You can admire someone not for their outcomes, but for their character. You can include them not for efficiency, but because their presence matters. You can let them lead in the places that light them up. You can give them room to stretch and change and dream again. You can offer steadiness when life is shaky, and reassurance when their own voice turns uncertain. You can remind them—when they forget—that they are still enough.

And then you can do it again.

The point of all this is not to become perfect. It is to become dependable. To become the kind of person others know they can return to—because even if you miss the moment today, you'll be looking for it tomorrow. Even if you fall into the old habits, you are building something new. And that rhythm, quiet and faithful, becomes the character of the relationship. It becomes what love sounds like. What love feels like. What love becomes.

That is what we've built together in these pages. Not a formula. Not a rulebook. But a rhythm. A way of seeing that invites us to care more precisely. To love more fully. To return more freely.

If you use it only for yourself, it will change how you love. If you offer it to the people you care about, it will change how they receive you. If you practise it together, even imperfectly, it will change how your relationships grow, endure, and heal.

Because love, at its best, is not made of rare gifts or poetic timing. It is made of recognitions. Small, repeated, refined over time. It is made of seeing what matters to someone—and choosing to make that part of how you love them. Not loudly. But reliably. Not perfectly. But consistently.

That is what love remembers.

And what it returns to.

Every time.

Start anywhere. Choose one need. Offer it often. Love will find its rhythm.

AFTERWORD

—— —— ✦ —— ——

I didn't learn these six needs from wisdom. I discovered them through failure — three long relationships, five, ten, and fifteen years — each teaching me, sometimes painfully, what I hadn't understood about giving and receiving love. And even now, I'm still learning. What I know today developed slowly, awkwardly, unevenly. It will for you too. That's part of the journey.

If you want to start, don't try to address all six needs at once. Begin with one relationship — the one you know best, maybe the closest, maybe the most challenging. Look for just one need in the other person. Observe, notice, guess if you need to: is it admiration they crave, belonging, control, freedom, security, or validation? Pick one. Focus on giving it genuinely, as often as you can. When it begins to feel natural — not yet a habit, but easier — add another. Build steadily. Over time, giving becomes instinctive, not effortful.

And be gentle with yourself. You will make mistakes. You

might offer the wrong gift at the wrong moment, or try so hard to "do it right" that sincerity gets lost in the effort. I've experienced all of that. Everyone does. But if you can forgive yourself for your mistakes, and forgive others theirs, something shifts. These are practices, not performances. They deepen over time.

To help you get started, here are some simple ideas for giving each of the six needs. These are not rules; they're starting points. Try them, discard what doesn't fit, and create your own. The point isn't perfection — it's noticing, choosing, and showing up.

Admiration

Admiration lives in the small things, though it shouldn't forget the big ones. Celebrate the milestones — the promotion, the achievement, the brave leap — but don't save your praise for rare events. Thank them for daily routines: the dishes, the meals, the laundry, earning a paycheck, picking up the kids. Quiet appreciation for the ordinary carries more meaning than distant applause. Say "I'm proud of you" often, and be specific — proud of their kindness, their effort, their patience, the difference they make. Offer compliments about who they are, not just what they do. And when you can, say it where others can hear.

Make it personal: Find the type of admiration that resonates most with them — quiet words, public praise, written notes — and speak it in their way.

Belonging

Belonging is built from small signals that say, "You matter here." Play games together and enjoy the game, not just the win. Watch their shows sometimes, or at least ask how the series is going. When you're together, put the phone down and be present. Save them a seat, include them in decisions, and bring them into moments that matter. And when they need you, make yourself available — even if it costs you focus or flow.

Make it personal: Ask yourself how they most like to be included — through touch, words, inside jokes, quiet rituals — and offer belonging in the way that feels right for them.

Control

Control in relationships isn't about authority — it's about trust. Let them lead, even in small things: driving, choosing, planning, deciding. And when they do, resist the urge to correct or improve their way of doing it. Smile, say something kind, or simply stay silent. Ask "What do you prefer?" before making shared decisions, and learn which areas matter most to them so they can steer where it counts.

Make it personal: Notice where they feel safest taking the lead and encourage their influence where it matters most.

Freedom

Freedom is the gift of letting someone grow into who they're becoming. Quietly notice something new today — something they say, or do, or like, or like to do. You don't always need to point it out; they'll feel your noticing anyway. Support one evolving dream, even if it surprises you. Celebrate changes instead of resisting them: "I love seeing you grow into this." Hold fewer assumptions about who they are or what they want; ask instead of guessing.

Make it personal: Find out what freedom means to them — space, trust, flexibility, new adventures — and offer it in the way they most need to receive it.

Security

Security grows from being someone they can count on. Be predictable in your reactions, especially when tensions rise. If you tend toward extremes, tame them: take a breath, take a walk, count to ten, listen before speaking. Unchecked anger, intimidation, or loudness have no place in a refuge. Keep small promises, every time. If they expect it, do it. Build rituals that anchor connection — a morning check-in, a shared phrase, an end-of-day debrief. And in conflict, signal "we" even when you disagree.

Make it personal: Learn what signals stability for them — daily texts, shared calendars, consistent tone — and build routines they can trust.

Validation

Validation quiets the fear of being "not enough." Don't correct, coach, teach, or fix unless you check in first: "Do you want my advice, or do you just want to figure it out?" Be the first to say "I love you." Be the first to apologise, the first to say "I was wrong," the first to ask forgiveness. Be the first to praise, encourage, and support. Catch moments of vulnerability and respond gently, without teasing or deflecting.

Make it personal: Learn where their quiet fears live — being unwanted, unseen, unworthy — and meet those fears with reassurance in the words that matter most to them.

One last thing: take care of your own needs, too. The people around you can't read your heart. Sometimes you'll have to teach them how to love you better — not through criticism or withdrawal, but through gratitude. When someone meets a need, even by accident, notice it, name it, and thank them. Encouragement is the strongest teacher; appreciation makes good patterns return. You shape the love you receive by celebrating the love you get.

And through all of it, be patient. Be compassionate — with them and with yourself. The work of love isn't in grand gestures; it's in the quiet rhythms that build refuge over time. A relationship becomes a safe place when we make it safe. Do that, and one day you'll look back and see that the small, steady gifts — offered again and again, until they became habit — were everything.

ALSO BY JIM VINCENT

---◆---

American Renewal
Volume I of *The American Renewal Trilogy*
A manifesto for resistance, a blueprint for survival, and a plan to outlast authoritarian rule. Written to confront the second Trump presidency with truth, clarity, and strategic resolve.

AMERICAN RESTORATION
Volume II of The American Renewal Trilogy
A comprehensive plan to rebuild the foundations of American democracy. Eighteen reforms necessary for rebuilding the foundations of democracy.

AMERICAN REDEMPTION
Volume III of *The American Renewal Trilogy*

Eighteen legislative reforms to fulfill the constitutional promises—justice, peace, defense, prosperity, liberty, and unity—and build a republic that serves all its people.

Essays on Tyranny

A collection of essays on the collapse of American political norms between 2000 and 2024, and the cultural, moral, and institutional choices that made authoritarianism possible.

Every Day: From Betrayal to Renewal

A strategic response to the 2025 "One Big Beautiful Bill," this book exposes its hidden harms and reframes its impact through nine democratic purposes—equipping readers with the facts, tools, and language to fight back.

The Quiet Habit of Giving

A book about love, loss, and repair. Based on the six emotional needs that sustain long relationships—Admiration, Belonging, Control, Freedom, Security, and Validation—and what happens when they are missing.

ABOUT THE AUTHOR

———✦———

Jim Vincent has spent a lifetime learning about love the hard way. Married four times—to three different women—and engaged once more, he thought at times that lasting connection might simply not be for him. One of those marriages, to Shelly, ended after ten years but never fully disappeared. Across decades and continents, the thread between them held. Eventually, they found their way back to each other, remarried, and began again—not from scratch, but from experience.

That experience shaped this book.

Drawing on years of failure, repair, and quiet rediscovery, *The Quiet Habit of Giving* reflects what Vincent learned about the emotional needs that make relationships endure—and the patterns that quietly undo them. He writes not as an expert, but as someone who kept trying, kept returning, and finally learned how to offer love in a way it could last.

Originally from the United States, Vincent now lives in Australia with his wife Shelly. He continues to write about love, belonging, and connection, alongside his broader work on democracy and social renewal.

You can find more of his work at https://jimvincent.us or https://jimvincentus.substack.com.

THANK YOU

Thank you for spending time with this book.

It was written slowly, through trial and return, shaped by the quiet work of trying to love better. If something in these pages spoke to you—if it helped you name a need, or offer one more gently to someone you care about—I'm grateful.

Love doesn't need to be perfect to last. It needs to be practiced. And the fact that you've come this far means you care enough to try. That matters more than you know.

If the book helped, I'd be honored if you shared it with someone else who might need it. And if you ever want to reach out, you can find me at https://jimvincent.us or https://jimvincentus.substack.com/

—JIM

www.ingramcontent.com/pod-product-compliance
Lightning Source LLC
Chambersburg PA
CBHW061212070526
44583CB00025B/3216